The Very Best of Thomas Jefferson

Thoughts of a Founding Father

DAVID GRAHAM

DISCLAIMER

Although every effort has been taken to ensure all information in this book is accurate, human error is always a possibility and therefore the author apologises in the event of any inaccuracies.

CONTENTS

Introduction   1

About America   3

About Freedom   7

About Himself   11

About Mankind   15

About War   21

General Thoughts & Opinions   25

God & Religion   31

Philosophy   35

Politics & Government   45

INTRODUCTION

As one of the founding fathers of America, and the third president, Thomas Jefferson is without doubt one of the most influential men in US history. His views transcended the world of politics and into the realms of philosophy.

Jefferson was outspoken on many topics, and would a fervent advocate of democracy and liberty. His expressions of freedom of religion for all were ahead of his time and his words are held to this day as fine teachings of justice and morality. Though he acknowledged the unfortunate necessity of war in certain cases, he was certainly against the principles of conflict and promoted the concept of peace among all.

Jefferson was openly opposed to the practice of slavery (despite owning many slaves himself, few of which he freed). It is in fact believed that he had a long term relationship with Sally Hemmings, one of his slaves, following the death of his wife. Some suggest that Jefferson was partly responsible for the eventual abolition of slavery due to his efforts, while in power, to advance legislation against it.

Generally known as one of the greatest US presidents of all time, from reading Jefferson's words it is easy to see why. His free thinking philosophy and overall respect for his fellow man is evident in much of what he said.

This book brings together some of the most interesting quotes from Jefferson to give you a further insight into the mind of one of the most important figures in American history.

ABOUT AMERICA

"When we get piled upon one another in large cities, as in Europe, we shall become as corrupt as Europe."

*

"The constitutions of most of our States assert that all power is inherent in the people; that... it is their right and duty to be at all times armed."

*

"If there is one principle more deeply rooted in the mind of every American, it is that we should have nothing to do with conquest."

*

"I am mortified to be told that, in the United States of America, the sale of a book can become a subject of inquiry, and of criminal inquiry too."

*

"The spirit of this country is totally adverse to a large military force."

*

"Peace and abstinence from European interferences are our objects, and so will continue while the present order of things in America remain uninterrupted."

*

"Our country is now taking so steady a course as to show by what road it will pass to destruction, to wit: by consolidation of power first, and then corruption, its necessary consequence."

ABOUT FREEDOM

"Educate and inform the whole mass of the people...
They are the only sure reliance for the preservation
of our liberty."

*

"We are not to expect to be translated from
despotism to liberty in a featherbed."

*

"Timid men prefer the calm of despotism to the
tempestuous sea of liberty."

*

"Rightful liberty is unobstructed action according to our will within limits drawn around us by the equal rights of others. I do not add 'within the limits of the law' because law is often but the tyrant's will, and always so when it violates the rights of the individual."

*

"The natural progress of things is for liberty to yield and government to gain ground."

*

"In every country and every age, the priest had been hostile to Liberty."

*

"No freeman shall be debarred the use of arms."

*

"The boisterous sea of liberty is never without a wave."

*

"Taste cannot be controlled by law."

*

"I would rather be exposed to the inconveniences attending too much liberty than those attending too small a degree of it."

*

"It behooves every man who values liberty of conscience for himself, to resist invasions of it in the case of others: or their case may, by change of circumstances, become his own."

*

"The tree of liberty must be refreshed from time to

time with the blood of patriots and tyrants."

*

"For a people who are free, and who mean to remain so, a well-organized and armed militia is their best security."

ABOUT HIMSELF

"There is not a sprig of grass that shoots
uninteresting to me."

*

"I never considered a difference of opinion in
politics, in religion, in philosophy, as cause for
withdrawing from a friend."

*

"I do not take a single newspaper, nor read one a
month, and I feel myself infinitely the happier for
it."

*

"I cannot live without books."

*

"My theory has always been, that if we are to dream, the flatteries of hope are as cheap, and pleasanter, than the gloom of despair."

*

"I am an Epicurean. I consider the genuine (not the imputed) doctrines of Epicurus as containing everything rational in moral philosophy which Greek and Roman leave to us."

*

"There is not a truth existing which I fear... or would wish unknown to the whole world."

*

"The glow of one warm thought is to me worth
more than money."

*

"I was bold in the pursuit of knowledge, never
fearing to follow truth and reason to whatever
results they led, and bearding every authority which
stood in their way."

*

"I like the dreams of the future better than the
history of the past."

*

"No occupation is so delightful to me as the culture
of the earth, and no culture comparable to that of
the garden."

*

13

"My only fear is that I may live too long. This would be a subject of dread to me."

ABOUT MANKIND

"The good opinion of mankind, like the lever of Archimedes, with the given fulcrum, moves the world."

*

"Only aim to do your duty, and mankind will give you credit where you fail."

*

"Peace and friendship with all mankind is our wisest policy, and I wish we may be permitted to pursue it."

*

"Nothing is unchangeable but the inherent and unalienable rights of man."

*

"The moment a person forms a theory, his imagination sees in every object only the traits which favor that theory."

*

"A coward is much more exposed to quarrels than a man of spirit."

*

"Power is not alluring to pure minds."

*

"Bodily decay is gloomy in prospect, but of all human contemplations the most abhorrent is body without mind."

*

"I sincerely believe... that banking establishments are more dangerous than standing armies."

*

"An association of men who will not quarrel with one another is a thing which has never yet existed, from the greatest confederacy of nations down to a town meeting or a vestry."

*

"There is a natural aristocracy among men. The grounds of this are virtue and talents."

*

"I find that he is happiest of whom the world says least, good or bad."

*

"One travels more usefully when alone, because he reflects more."

*

"When a man assumes a public trust he should consider himself a public property."

*

"I believe that every human mind feels pleasure in doing good to another."

*

"It takes time to persuade men to do even what is for their own good."

*

"Mankind are more disposed to suffer, while evils
are sufferable, than to right themselves by
abolishing the forms to which they are
accustomed."

*

"Nothing gives one person so much advantage over
another as to remain always cool and unruffled
under all circumstances."

*

"An injured friend is the bitterest of foes."

*

"The man who reads nothing at all is better
educated than the man who reads nothing but
newspapers."

*

"Every citizen should be a soldier. This was the
case with the Greeks and Romans, and must be that

of every free state."

*

"The natural cause of the human mind is certainly from credulity to skepticism."

*

"Whenever a man has cast a longing eye on offices, a rottenness begins in his conduct."

*

"Experience demands that man is the only animal which devours his own kind, for I can apply no milder term to the general prey of the rich on the poor."

*

"Nothing can stop the man with the right mental attitude from achieving his goal; nothing on earth can help the man with the wrong mental attitude."

ABOUT WAR

"I think with the Romans, that the general of today should be a soldier tomorrow if necessary."

*

"In defense of our persons and properties under actual violation, we took up arms. When that violence shall be removed, when hostilities shall cease on the part of the aggressors, hostilities shall cease on our part also."

*

"The most successful war seldom pays for its

losses."

*

"War is an instrument entirely inefficient toward redressing wrong; and multiplies, instead of indemnifying losses."

*

"An enemy generally says and believes what he wishes."

*

"As our enemies have found we can reason like men, so now let us show them we can fight like men also."

*

"One loves to possess arms, though they hope never to have occasion for them."

*

"I abhor war and view it as the greatest scourge of mankind."

*

"We did not raise armies for glory or for conquest."

*

"None but an armed nation can dispense with a standing army. To keep ours armed and disciplined is therefore at all times important."

*

"I have seen enough of one war never to wish to see another."

*

"Friendship is but another name for an alliance with the follies and the misfortunes of others. Our own

share of miseries is sufficient: why enter then as
volunteers into those of another?"

GENERAL THOUGHTS & OPINIONS

"It is our duty still to endeavor to avoid war; but if it shall actually take place, no matter by whom brought on, we must defend ourselves. If our house be on fire, without inquiring whether it was fired from within or without, we must try to extinguish it."

*

"No duty the Executive had to perform was so trying as to put the right man in the right place."

*

"We never repent of having eaten too little."

*

"Merchants have no country. The mere spot they stand on does not constitute so strong an attachment as that from which they draw their gains."

*

"A strong body makes the mind strong. As to the species of exercises, I advise the gun. While this gives moderate exercise to the body, it gives boldness, enterprise and independence to the mind. Games played with the ball, and others of that nature, are too violent for the body and stamp no character on the mind. Let your gun therefore be your constant companion of your walks."

*

"We may consider each generation as a distinct nation, with a right, by the will of its majority, to bind themselves, but none to bind the succeeding generation, more than the inhabitants of another country."

*

"Walking is the best possible exercise. Habituate yourself to walk very far."

*

"Where the press is free and every man able to read, all is safe."

*

"Leave all the afternoon for exercise and recreation, which are as necessary as reading. I will rather say more necessary because health is worth more than learning."

*

"Books constitute capital. A library book lasts as long as a house, for hundreds of years. It is not, then, an article of mere consumption but fairly of capital, and often in the case of professional men, setting out in life, it is their only capital."

*

"If a nation expects to be ignorant and free, in a state of civilization, it expects what never was and never will be."

*

"All, too, will bear in mind this sacred principle, that though the will of the majority is in all cases to prevail, that will to be rightful must be reasonable; that the minority possess their equal rights, which equal law must protect, and to violate would be oppression."

*

"Advertisements contain the only truths to be relied on in a newspaper."

*

"The whole commerce between master and slave is a perpetual exercise of the most boisterous passions, the most unremitting despotism on the one part, and degrading submissions on the other. Our children see this, and learn to imitate it."

*

"Commerce with all nations, alliance with none, should be our motto."

*

"The world is indebted for all triumphs which have been gained by reason and humanity over error and oppression."

*

"Peace, commerce and honest friendship with all nations; entangling alliances with none."

GOD & RELIGION

"The way to silence religious disputes is to take no notice of them."

*

"I have sworn upon the altar of God, eternal hostility against every form of tyranny over the mind of man."

*

"The God who gave us life, gave us liberty at the same time."

*

"It is in our lives and not our words that our religion must be read."

*

"To compel a man to furnish funds for the propagation of ideas he disbelieves and abhors is sinful and tyrannical."

*

"It is always better to have no ideas than false ones; to believe nothing, than to believe what is wrong."

*

"The Creator has not thought proper to mark those in the forehead who are of stuff to make good generals. We are first, therefore, to seek them blindfold, and then let them learn the trade at the expense of great losses."

*

"I tremble for my country when I reflect that God is just; that his justice cannot sleep forever."

*

"Difference of opinion is advantageous in religion. The several sects perform the office of a Censor - over each other."

*

"It does me no injury for my neighbor to say there are twenty gods or no God."

*

"Fix reason firmly in her seat, and call to her tribunal every fact, every opinion. Question with boldness even the existence of a God; because, if there be one, he must more approve of the homage of reason, than that of blindfolded fear."

*

"I never will, by any word or act, bow to the shrine of intolerance or admit a right of inquiry into the religious opinions of others."

*

"We hold these truths to be self-evident: that all men are created equal; that they are endowed by their Creator with certain unalienable rights; that among these are life, liberty, and the pursuit of happiness."

*

"If God is just, I tremble for my country."

PHILOSOPHY

"Happiness is not being pained in body or troubled in mind."

*

"He who knows nothing is closer to the truth than he whose mind is filled with falsehoods and errors."

*

"He who knows best knows how little he knows."

*

"Do you want to know who you are? Don't ask. Act! Action will delineate and define you."

*

"How much pain they have cost us, the evils which have never happened."

*

"Truth is certainly a branch of morality and a very important one to society."

*

"Do not bite at the bait of pleasure, till you know there is no hook beneath it."

*

"Don't talk about what you have done or what you are going to do."

*

"Our greatest happiness does not depend on the condition of life in which chance has placed us, but is always the result of a good conscience, good health, occupation, and freedom in all just pursuits."

*

"The earth belongs to the living, not to the dead."

*

"It is neither wealth nor splendor; but tranquility and occupation which give you happiness."

*

"In matters of style, swim with the current; in matters of principle, stand like a rock."

*

"Resort is had to ridicule only when reason is against us."

*

"Never spend your money before you have earned it."

*

"Delay is preferable to error."

*

"One man with courage is a majority."

*

"But friendship is precious, not only in the shade, but in the sunshine of life, and thanks to a benevolent arrangement the greater part of life is sunshine."

*

"Whenever you do a thing, act as if all the world were watching."

*

"It is more dangerous that even a guilty person should be punished without the forms of law than that he should escape."

*

"Honesty is the first chapter in the book of wisdom."

*

"Errors of opinion may be tolerated where reason is left free to combat it."

*

"When angry count to ten before you speak. If very angry, count to one hundred."

*

"Be polite to all, but intimate with few."

*

"Wisdom I know is social. She seeks her fellows.
But Beauty is jealous, and illy bears the presence of
a rival."

*

"I hope our wisdom will grow with our power, and
teach us, that the less we use our power the greater
it will be."

*

"Determine never to be idle. No person will have
occasion to complain of the want of time who never
loses any. It is wonderful how much may be done if
we are always doing."

*

"Ignorance is preferable to error, and he is less remote from the truth who believes nothing than he who believes what is wrong."

*

"To penetrate and dissipate these clouds of darkness, the general mind must be strengthened by education."

*

"Always take hold of things by the smooth handle."

*

"Force is the vital principle and immediate parent of despotism."

*

"It is incumbent on every generation to pay its own

debts as it goes. A principle which if acted on would save one-half the wars of the world."

*

"Speeches that are measured by the hour will die with the hour."

*

"Money, not morality, is the principle commerce of civilized nations."

*

"Enlighten the people generally, and tyranny and oppressions of body and mind will vanish like evil spirits at the dawn of day."

*

"Dependence begets subservience and venality, suffocates the germ of virtue, and prepares fit tools for the designs of ambition."

*

"In truth, politeness is artificial good humor, it covers the natural want of it, and ends by rendering habitual a substitute nearly equivalent to the real virtue."

POLITICS & GOVERNMENT

"Politics is such a torment that I advise everyone I love not to mix with it."

*

"The spirit of resistance to government is so valuable on certain occasions that I wish it to be always kept alive."

*

"If we can but prevent the government from wasting the labours of the people, under the pretence of taking care of them, they must become happy."

*

"I know of no safe depository of the ultimate powers of the society but the people themselves; and if we think them not enlightened enough to exercise their control with a wholesome discretion, the remedy is not to take it from them but to inform their discretion."

*

"I have no fear that the result of our experiment will be that men may be trusted to govern themselves without a master."

*

"I own that I am not a friend to a very energetic government. It is always oppressive."

*

"A Bill of Rights is what the people are entitled to against every government, and what no just government should refuse, or rest on inference."

*

"I have no ambition to govern men; it is a painful and thankless office."

*

"I hope we shall crush in its birth the aristocracy of our monied corporations which dare already to challenge our government to a trial by strength, and bid defiance to the laws of our country."

*

"Sometimes it is said that man cannot be trusted with the government of himself. Can he, then be trusted with the government of others? Or have we found angels in the form of kings to govern him? Let history answer this question."

*

"Experience hath shewn, that even under the best

forms of government those entrusted with power have, in time, and by slow operations, perverted it into tyranny."

*

"That government is the strongest of which every man feels himself a part."

*

"Conquest is not in our principles. It is inconsistent with our government."

*

"If the present Congress errs in too much talking, how can it be otherwise in a body to which the people send one hundred and fifty lawyers, whose trade it is to question everything, yield nothing, and talk by the hour?"

*

"Every government degenerates when trusted to the

rulers of the people alone. The people themselves are its only safe depositories."

*

"It is error alone which needs the support of government. Truth can stand by itself."

*

"Were it left to me to decide whether we should have a government without newspapers, or newspapers without a government, I should not hesitate a moment to prefer the latter."

*

"So confident am I in the intentions, as well as wisdom, of the government, that I shall always be satisfied that what is not done, either cannot, or ought not to be done."

*

"History, in general, only informs us of what bad

government is."

*

"No man will ever carry out of the Presidency the reputation which carried him into it."

*

"The republican is the only form of government which is not eternally at open or secret war with the rights of mankind."

*

"A wise and frugal government, which shall restrain men from injuring one another, shall leave them otherwise free to regulate their own pursuits of industry and improvement, and shall not take from the mouth of labor the bread it has earned."

*

"The care of human life and happiness, and not their destruction, is the first and only object of good government."

*

"The second office in the government is honorable and easy; the first is but a splendid misery."

*

"No government ought to be without censors; and where the press is free no one ever will."

*

"Whenever the people are well-informed, they can be trusted with their own government."

*

"Leave no authority existing not responsible to the people."

ALSO BY DAVID GRAHAM

The Philosophy of Mark Twain

The Very Best of Friedrich Nietzsche

Inside the Mind of George Bernard Shaw

The Very Best of Ralph Waldo Emerson

The Very Best of Clint Eastwood

The Very Best of Roger Moore

The Very Best of Kirk Douglas